O9-BTZ-920

A Young Citizen's Guide to News Literacy

VIRAL NEWS ON SOCIAL MEDIA

Paul Lane

PowerKiDS
press™
New York

Published in 2019 by The Rosen Publishing Group, Inc.
29 East 21st Street, New York, NY 10010

First Edition

Editor: Jill Keppeler
Book Design: Reann Nye

Photo Credits: Cover Uber Images/Shutterstock.com; p. 4 michaeljung/Shutterstock.com; p. 5 Vasin Lee/Shutterstock.com; pp. 7, 24 Rawpixel.com/Shutterstock.com; p. 9 Bloomberg/Getty Images; p. 11 Andrew Lichtenstein/Corbis News/Getty Images; p. 12 Roman Samborskyi/Shutterstock.com; p. 13 DANIEL SORABJI/AFP/Getty Images; p. 15 NurPhoto/Getty Images; p. 17 STR/AFP/Getty Images; p. 19 KAREN BLEIER/AFP/Getty Images; p. 21 NICHOLAS KAMM/AFP/Getty Images; p. 23 temizyurek/iStock Unreleased/Getty Images; p. 25 Chip Somodevilla/ Getty Images News/Getty Images; p. 27 Tempura/E+/Getty Images; p. 28 JGI/Jamie Grill/ Blend Images/Getty Images; p. 29 REDPIXEL.PL/ Shutterstock.com; p. 30 LeoPatrizi/E+/Getty Images.

Cataloging-in-Publishing Data

Names: Lane, Paul.
Title: Viral news on social media / Paul Lane.
Description: New York : PowerKids Press, 2019. | Series: A young citizen's guide to news literacy | Includes glossary and index.
Identifiers: ISBN 9781538346181 (pbk.) | ISBN 9781538345030 (library bound) | ISBN 9781538346198 (6 pack)
Subjects: LCSH: Social media–Juvenile literature. | User-generated content–Juvenile literature. | Digital media–Juvenile literature.
Classification: LCC HM742.L36 2019 | DDC 302.23'1–dc23

Manufactured in the United States of America

CPSIA Compliance Information: Batch #CWPK19. For Further Information contact Rosen Publishing, New York, New York at 1-800-237-9932

CONTENTS

READER BEWARE 4

TOO FAST, TOO FALSE? 6

FEELING SOCIAL 8

HOW DOES NEWS GET SICK? 10

HOW CAN NEWS BE FAKE? 12

SPREADING LIES 14

BLAME THE BOTS 16

WHAT'S THE DIFFERENCE? 18

IT'S NOT ALWAYS GOOD TO SHARE 20

SO MUCH INFORMATION 22

FIGHTING BACK 24

WHOM DO YOU TRUST? 26

WHEN IN DOUBT, DON'T SEND IT OUT 28

IS THAT CLEAR? 30

GLOSSARY 31

INDEX 32

WEBSITES 32

READER BEWARE

Whether it's the latest update about the president or the newest superhero movie, some news stories are almost unavoidable. With or without the author's intent, some stories will be shared across every screen connected to the Internet and praised (or complained about) on every social media site. But is that a good thing?

That depends. When a story is true, has real meaning, and is important to readers' (or viewers') lives, then it's for the better that more people consume it. But when someone creates a story just to bring shame to someone else or hurt their cause—something often done using lies or untruths— it's wise to hesitate when deciding whether to share.

How can you tell the difference? Read on to find out.

Social media has become a common part of American life. Users should be aware, though, that many people and companies are out there trying to trick them on social media.

5

Tuu Fast, Tuu False?

Social media makes it a lot easier for people to spread news quickly, sometimes without even stopping to think about it. Social media sites such as Facebook, Twitter, and Instagram allow users to connect with friends, family members, coworkers, and anyone else. Users often share tidbits from their lives, along with pictures, videos, and news stories they're interested in.

The way users feel about those stories, though, often is a big part of what they choose to share. Baseball fans may share Yankees or Mets stories, while Republicans and Democrats may share stories supporting their political views. All it takes is a quick click or two. That speed can keep people from stopping to judge the quality of the story or its truth. That's a big part of the problem.

BREAKING NEWS

The world has an estimated 2.62 billion social media users as of 2018, up from 970 million at the start of the decade. Facebook is the most popular site.

The world has billions of social media users. Many simply look to see what's going on in others' lives, but social media is also a big source of news.

FEELING SOCIAL

Sites and apps that started as simple ways to share information have become big business for social media companies. At least six companies are worth more than $1 billion, with Facebook worth more than $500 billion. One of the earliest social media sites, MySpace, sold for $580 million in 2005.

The people running these sites rely on advertising money. In the United States and Canada alone, businesses spent about $15 billion to advertise on social media sites in 2017—about three times what they spent in 2013. That breaks down to more than $50 for each user in those countries.

It's therefore very important for social media sites to maintain their numbers and grow, as more users will mean more targets for advertisers.

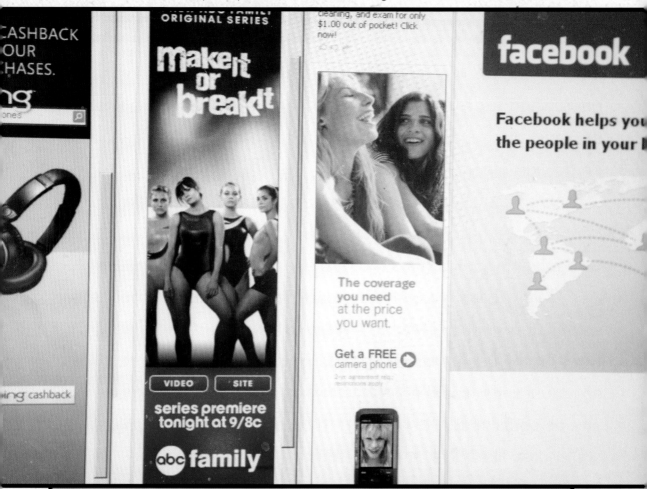

Advertisers spend billions of dollars on Facebook and other social media sites. That puts pressure on sites to grow their user bases.

MORE DATA, MORE PROBLEMS

Companies might want information on social media users for more than just advertising. Facebook was sued in 2018 for not stopping data company Cambridge Analytica from using information from more than 71 million Facebook users as part of a targeted political campaign. Cambridge Analytica **allegedly** used the information to figure out which users would most likely vote for Donald Trump when he ran for president in 2016 and to target them with specific pro-Trump ads and news.

HOW DOES NEWS GET SICK?

The term "viral news" refers to stories that spread very quickly and widely over the Internet. Some of the stories shared the most offer shock value that matches the sharers' viewpoints on politics, life, or other matters.

Copycat sites made only to repost stories reported in other places make things worse. The people running these sites take advantage of stories that are already becoming popular.

Many times, a picture or headline that misleads about the actual story is all it takes for a story to be shared, regardless of whether the user reads the article. This helps news spread like an actual virus would spread between people, some experts say, as social media users tend to be connected to people who are equally likely to share the story.

BREAKING NEWS

An **analysis** of Facebook data found fake news stories about crime and politics were more widely shared in 2017 than in the year before. A lot of these stories came from sites made just for fake news.

Fake news isn't new, but its rapid growth on social media and across the Internet means it can move faster and mislead more people than ever before.

HOW CAN NEWS BE FAKE?

Fake news is pretty much what it sounds like—news stories that are lies. The writers create them knowing this. But why lie about the news?

The simple answers: it's profitable and it's a way to advance a cause. Many website owners get paid on a per-click basis, so the more clicks they get, the more money comes in. Some website owners and writers care more about that than telling the truth. The more shocking their stories are, the more clicks they'll get.

Other writers want to make readers come around to their point of view, so they write stories that are meant to turn people against certain leaders and ideas. They may lie about people committing crimes or otherwise acting in ways that would make supporters reject them.

False news is often meant to get readers angry, usually in an attempt to get them to like something or dislike something else.

WHY FAKE NEWS IS A PROBLEM

Fake news has real consequences. One fake news story claimed that Hillary Clinton ran a criminal operation in a pizza shop before the 2016 presidential election. A man believed the story and shot a gun into the shop. Another fake news story claimed the flu shot for the 2017–18 flu season actually made people sick. This convinced some readers not to get a flu shot, although it's really the best way to avoid the flu.

13

SPREADING LIES

Anyone who's ever told or shared a lie knows how easily lies spread, whether it's at school, at home, or anywhere else. Sometimes people would rather believe what's shocking but wrong than believe what's boring but true—an idea that's backed up by a study published in 2018 by the Massachusetts Institute of **Technology**.

That study found that fake stories spread on Twitter six times faster than true ones, and lies are 70 percent more likely to be shared than true stories. Those shares could come all at once or more slowly, a few users at a time.

Human nature surely plays a role in spreading lies. But the people most interested in spreading lies usually get some help from technology in ruining the truth.

BREAKING NEWS

Even governments get in on the act. A study released in 2017 found that some governments have social media accounts that are used for spreading fake news.

Fake news writers know users are more likely to pay attention to shocking headlines, regardless of their truth.

BLAME THE BOTS

Many social media users set up bots to help spread information. Bots (short for "robots") are **automated** systems that can follow users, create posts, and share others' posts. Many of these accounts are set up for a specific purpose, whether to back one person or movement or to bring down another.

Twitter, for example, has about 15 percent bot-run accounts (including government accounts that send weather and other alerts). Those bots can be taught to share useful information, but they can also be taught to seek and share lies. Accounts may equally share real and fake news, but the fact that lies can be shared without a real person actually doing anything makes the problem harder to control. Bots may account for up to half of all Internet traffic.

BREAKING NEWS

In 2018, Twitter announced steps to limit the effect that bots can have on the social media platform. The site is limiting the ability to share stories and links across multiple accounts.

There are signs you can use to figure out whether a
social media account is run by a bot. If you find a bot,
you can report it—or just ignore it.

SPOT THE BOT

Looking for bots on social media? Check the account information. Does the information sound like a real person wrote it? Does the account have a profile picture? If you search that picture, does it seem to be **unique**? Those are signs of a real account. Does the account post every few minutes over a whole day? Does it seem to share a lot of **controversial** news? Those are warning signs.

17

WHAT'S THE DIFFERENCE?

Real news tends to come from trusted sources where real fact-checking takes place. This includes news outlets such as the *New York Times* and NBC, magazines such as *Time*, and public radio. These sources will **verify** facts and usually won't let a story run if the facts can't be proven. Good news sources also correct stories found to have problems. Some websites can also be good news sources.

Websites with a noted **slant**, however, may not be. Some sites tend to print stories that may use little or no facts to back up their accusations. How can you tell the difference? Balanced stories that **cite** good information sources, such as real experts on a subject, and provide real names and contact information are more likely to be true.

BREAKING NEWS

If anything is labeled as "opinion," read it cautiously. Since opinions reflect how a person feels about something, they can't be false, but they can be based on false information.

Trusted news is more likely to come from traditional sources such as newspapers and established TV channels—those that employ fact-checkers and other people who verify information.

IT'S NOT ALWAYS GOOD TO SHARE

It's important to make sure the news you share is true. Truthful news sources will generally represent the story in the headline or opening sentence, as opposed to a catchy teaser line meant to compel you to click a link. (Think "You won't believe how he responded to THAT!")

Real news can be interesting, but if you find yourself getting upset about something you read, you should probably take a step back and think. Fake news tends to create **outrage** that will make the reader want to share it—without actually reading the story, if possible. (That lets a story spread faster.) You can also check to see if the story is being reported elsewhere, as truth tends to be picked up by a lot of **credible** outlets.

BREAKING NEWS

Twitter accounts with a checkmark next to the name are verified accounts. This means the account has been proven to represent that person. These are more trustworthy.

Social media sites will often verify popular accounts that share news. That's meant to tell fellow users that the person/source is real and credible.

verified account

TWEETS
556

FOLLOWING
448

A Ve

Tweets   Tweets

Pinned Tweet

Tim Armstrong

Billion+

Unstopp

Tim Armstrong ✔

@timarmstrongaol

Autodidact / Teammate / Building Brands People ♥ / Boston Sports Fanatic

aol.com

SNOPES HAS THE SCOOPS

Another way to figure out whether what you're seeing is worth believing is to visit a fact-checking site such as Snopes.com. This site is dedicated to checking stories, including items that are often shared on social media. This includes news stories, memes, and videos. Other dependable fact-checking sites include FactCheck.org, Politifact.com, and the *Washington Post*'s Fact Checker blog.

SO MUCH INFORMATION

Social media has been a product of—and has helped to grow—the 24-hour news cycle, in which TV networks and online resources have to create content and fill space nonstop. With constant competition for content, news producers and online sites have to produce new things to cut through the sea of information and get themselves noticed.

That's created a more **sensational** take on many news stories. Instead of just telling the story, some news sources turn to increased drama to encourage more consumers to stay tuned in, listening, or reading. In some cases, that's led to networks with people actually shouting at each other on screen to draw attention. In others, it encourages less fact-checking and more reliance on sharply worded opinion.

BREAKING NEWS

CNN, which started in 1980, was the first 24-hour news network. By the turn of the 21st century, there were dozens of 24-hour networks, including some focused on individual cities or areas.

The 24-hour news cycle is now a permanent part of American life. With so many ways to continuously share information, news agencies are under pressure to fill that never-ending gap.

FIGHTING BACK

Social media site owners have begun fighting back against bad information shared on their sites. Facebook started asking users which sites they trust more so that the less trusted ones could be weeded out. Twitter and Tumblr banned questionable accounts—including some run by a Russian organization that was spreading lies and misinformation—and reached out to users who had interacted with them.

Facebook took more steps a couple months later, including adding links to reputable sites that verify information in shared stories and facts about the news outlets that put out the stories. The hope is to show users how to pick out which stories are likely to be fake news before those stories can go viral—and out of control.

After the Cambridge Analytica problem, Facebook founder Mark Zuckerberg had to speak before Congress in April 2018. He said his company would do better at protecting user data.

PLUGGING IN

The Internet has become the primary way of obtaining news for many people. The Pew Research Center found that websites and news apps—including those run by traditional print and broadcast companies—were the most popular delivery method for news in 2017. Social media was a close second and was also the fastest-growing news source from 2012 to 2017, according to the Reuters Institute.

WHoM dU YoU TRUsT?

The amount of information out there makes it easy for some people to stop trusting the media. Two-thirds of those who responded to a poll in 2016 said they distrusted traditional news media, a rise from 53 percent in 1997. This is further divided along political lines, something that may be made worse by people who use "fake news" to describe news they don't like.

The most reputable news sources tend not to take sides in news stories. They're more willing to answer questions about stories and correct any mistakes. Reputable news outlets also have easily found codes of **ethics** for their employees to follow and standards for those employees. Those who don't follow these standards may be fired or forced to resign.

People tend to believe what they want to believe.
It's important to look at facts.

27

WHEN IN DOUBT, DON'T SEND IT OUT

If you want to avoid sharing fake news that's gone viral, there are a couple things you can do. The easiest is to actually read or watch the story before sharing it. A recent study found that 60 percent of social media users would share a story without actually reading the story first. That study included, in one test, a story with a scary headline that had nonsense as the body.

Another thing you can do is simplify your news sources. Another study found that people who read more news on social media are more likely to share fake news, in part because they are reading too much to focus on one thing and fully consider it. These findings point to one good rule: if you aren't sure whether you should share something, don't.

Social media users should think twice about what they're reading or watching before sharing it. They should also make sure they understand what they're sharing.

IS THAT CLEAR?

When it comes to identifying viral news on social media, the key is to think about what you see. Don't fall for a catchy headline—think critically and ask yourself a few questions. Does this seem like it could actually happen? Does this lack an obvious slant in opinion? Does this have a headline that provides real information? If you can answer yes to all those questions, the item can likely be trusted. If not, you may have fake news in front of you.

The truth is out there, but the emphasis is on all news consumers to find it—a task that's easier said than done. Stay determined and open minded, and you'll always find yourself on the good side of any social media conversation.

GLOSSARY

alleged: Asserted to be true or to exist.

analysis: A careful study or explanation of something.

automated: To be able to run on its own.

cite: To name something used, such as a source.

controversial: Likely to give rise to disagreement.

credible: Reliable, believable.

ethics: Rules based on what's right and what's wrong.

outrage: Extreme anger or a great sense of unhappiness because of something that's wrong.

sensational: Created to draw much interest; often shocking.

slant: A way in which something is presented that favors a certain group or opinion.

technology: A method that uses science to solve problems and the tools used to solve those problems.

unique: Special or different from anything else.

verify: To make sure something is true.

INDEX

A

advertisers, 8, 9

B

bots, 16, 17

C

Cambridge Analytica, 9, 25
Canada, 8
Clinton, Hillary, 13
CNN, 22

F

Facebook, 6, 8, 9, 10, 24, 25, 30
fact-checkers, 18, 19, 21, 22

I

Instagram, 6
Internet, 4, 10, 11

M

Massachusetts Institute of Technology (MIT), 14

N

NBC, 18
New York Times, 18

P

Pew Research Center, 25

R

Reuters Institute, 25

T

Time, 18
Trump, Donald, 9
Tumblr, 24
24-hour news cycle, 22, 23
Twitter, 6, 14, 16, 20, 24

U

United States, 8

V

verification, 20, 21, 24
viral news, 10

Z

Zuckerberg, Mark, 25

WEBSITES

Due to the changing nature of Internet links, PowerKids Press has developed an online list of websites related to the subject of this book. This site is updated regularly. Please use this link to access the list: www.powerkidslinks.com/newslit/viral